A Little Treasury of
HAIKU

A Little Treasury of
HAIKU

*Basho, Buson, Issa, Shiki,
Sokan, Kikaku, and others*

Translated by Peter Beilenson

AVENEL BOOKS

New York

Inquiries should be addressed to:
Peter Pauper Press
135 West 50th Street
New York, N.Y. 10020

This edition is published by Avenel Books,
distributed by Crown Publishers, Inc.,
by arrangement with Peter Pauper Press.
a b c d e f g h
AVENEL 1980 EDITION

Manufactured in the United States of America

Library of Congress Cataloging in Publication Data
Main entry under title:

A little treasury of haiku.

1. Haiku--Translations into English. 2. English
poetry--Translations from Japanese. I. Matsuo,
Basho, 1644-1694. II. Beilenson, Peter, 1905-1962.
PL782.E3L5 1980   895.6'104'08   80-17715
ISBN: 0-517-320967

A NOTE ON JAPANESE HAIKU

THE *hokku*—or more properly *haiku*—is a tiny verse-form in which Japanese poets have been working for hundreds of years. Originally it was the first part of the *tanka,* a five-line poem, often written by two people as a literary game: one writing three lines, the other, two lines capping them. But the *hokku,* or three-line starting verse, became popular as a separate form. As such it is properly called *haiku,* and retains an incredible popularity among all classes of Japanese.

There are only seventeen syllables in the *haiku,* the first and third lines contain five, the second line seven. There is almost always in it the name of the season, or a key word giving the season by inference. (This is a short-cut, costing the poet only one or two syllables, whereby the reader can immediately comprehend the weather, the foliage, the bird and insect-life— and the emotions traditional to the season: factors which almost always are important in the poem.) But there is also, in a good *haiku,* more than a mere statement of feeling or a picture of nature: there is an implied identity between two seemingly different things.

The greatest of *haiku*-writers, and the poet who crystallized the style, was Basho

(1644-1694). In his later years he was a student of Zen Buddhism, and his later poems, which are his best, express the rapturous awareness in that mystical philosophy of the identity of life in all its forms. With this awareness, Basho immersed himself in even the tiniest things, and with religious fervor and sure craftsmanship converted them into poetry. He was ardently loved by his followers, and by later poets, and his Zen philosophy has thus been perpetuated in later *haiku*. It is, indeed, a key to the completest appreciation of most *haiku*.

Following Basho in time and fame was Buson (1715-1783)—a little more sophisticated and detached than his predecessor, and an equally exquisite craftsman. The third great *haiku* poet was unhappy Issa (1763-1827), a continual butt of fate. He is less poetic but more lovable than Basho and Buson. His tender, witty *haiku* about his dead children, his bitter poverty, his little insect friends, endear him to every reader. Other masters are of course represented here too.

It is usually impossible to translate a *haiku* literally and have it remain a poem, or remain in the proper seventeen-syllable form. There are several reasons for this. *Haiku* are full of quotations and allusions which are recognized by literate Japanese but not by us; and are full of

6

interior double-meanings almost like James Joyce. And the language is used without connecting-words or tenses or pronouns or indications or singular or plural—almost a telegraphic form. Obviously a translation cannot be at once so illusive and so terse.

In the *texture* of the poems there is a further difficulty: Japanese is highly polysyllabic. The only way to reproduce such a texture in English is to use Latinized words—normally less sympathetic than the Anglo-Saxon. For all these reasons, the following versions make no pretense to be literal or complete, and some variations in the five-seven-five syllable arrangements have been allowed.

Alterations and interior rhymes, which are common in Japanese because every syllable ends with one of the five vowel sounds (sometimes with the addition of the letter "n") have been freely used; but as in the originals, there are no end-rhymes except some accidental ones.

One final word: the *haiku* is not expected to be always a complete or even a clear statement. The reader is supposed to add to the words his own associations and imagery, and thus to become a co-creator of his own pleasure in the poem. The publishers hope their readers may here co-create such pleasure for themselves!

In these dark waters
Drawn up from my frozen well . . .
Glittering of spring
RINGAI

Standing still at dusk
Listen . . . in far distances
The song of froglings!
BUSON

I dreamed of battles
And was slain . . . oh savage samurai!
Insatiable fleas!
KIKAKU

Year's first cart-load . . .
Cut-out paper flowers deck
The emaciated horse
SHIKI

8

In silent mid-night
Our old scarecrow topples down . . .
Weird hollow echo
BONCHO

Women planting rice . . .
Ugly every bit about them . . .
But their ancient song
RAIZAN

Wild geese write a line
Flap-flapping across the sky . . .
Comical Dutch script
SOIN

Dead my old fine hopes
And dry my dreaming but still . . .
Iris, blue each spring
SHUSHIKI

In this windy nest
Open your hungry mouth in vain . . .
Issa, stepchild bird
ISSA

9

Ballet in the air . . .
Twin butterflies until, twice white
They meet, they mate
BASHO

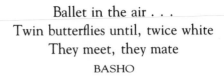

ON THE DEATH OF HIS CHILD
Dew evaporates
And all our world is dew . . . so dear,
So fresh, so fleeting
ISSA

Black cloudbank broken
Scatters in the night . . . now see
Moon-lighted mountains!
BASHO

Seek on high bare trails
Sky-reflecting violets . . .
Mountain-top jewels
BASHO

For a lovely bowl
Let us arrange these flowers . . .
Since there is no rice
BASHO

Now that eyes of hawks
In dusky night are darkened . . .
Chirping of the quails
BASHO

My two plum trees are
So gracious . . . see, they flower
One now, one later
BUSON

One fallen flower
Returning to the branch? . . . oh no!
A white butterfly
MORITAKE

Cloudbank curling low?
Ah! the mountain Yoshino . . .
Cherry cumulus!
RYOTA

Fie! this fickle world!
Three days, neglected cherry-branch . . .
And you are bare
RYOTA

11

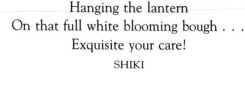

Hanging the lantern
On that full white blooming bough . . .
Exquisite your care!

SHIKI

April's air stirs in
Willow-leaves . . . a butterfly
Floats and balances

BASHO

In the sea-surf edge
Mingling with bright small shells . . .
Bush-clover petals

BASHO

THE RIVER
Gathering May rains
From cold streamlets for the sea . . .
Murmuring Mogami

BASHO

A gate made all of twigs
With woven grass for hinges . . .
For a lock . . . this snail

ISSA

Wind-blown, rained on . . .
Bent barley-grass you make me
Narrow path indeed
JOSO

Arise from sleep, old cat,
And with great yawns and
stretchings . . . amble out for love
ISSA

White cloud of mist
Above white cherry-blossoms . . .
Dawn-shining mountains
BASHO

Hi! my little hut
Is newly-thatched I see . . . .
Blue morning-glories
ISSA

In the city fields
Contemplating cherry-trees . . .
Strangers are like friends
ISSA

See, see, see! oh see!
Oh what to say? ah Yoshino . . .
Mountain-all-abloom!
TEISHITSU

Green shadow-dances . . .
See our young banana-tree
Pattering the screen
SHIKI

Don't touch my plumtree!
Said my friend and saying so . . .
Broke the branch for me
TAIGI

Twilight whippoorwill . . .
Whistle on, sweet deepener
Of dark loneliness
BASHO

Reciting scriptures . . .
Strange the wondrous blue I find
In morning-glories
KYOROKU

14

Many solemn nights
Blond moon, we stand and marvel . . .
Sleeping our noons away
TEITOKU

Mountain-rose petals
Falling, falling, falling now . . .
Waterfall music
BASHO

Amorous cat, alas
You too must yowl with your love . . .
Or even worse, without!
YAHA

The laden wagon runs
Bumbling and creaking down the road . . .
Three peonies tremble
BUSON

Ah me! I am one
Who spends his little breakfast
Morning-glory gazing
BASHO

My good father raged
When I snapped the peony . . .
Precious memory!

TAIRO

By that fallen house
The pear-tree stands full-blooming . . .
An ancient battle-site

SHIKI

In the open shop
Paperweights on picture books . . .
Young springtime breeze

KITO

Dim the grey cow comes
Mooing mooing and mooing
Out of the morning mist

ISSA

Take the round flat moon
Snap this twig for handle . . .
What a pretty fan!

SOKAN

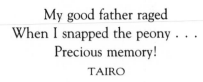

16

Seas are wild tonight . . .
Stretching over Sado Island
Silent clouds of stars
BASHO

Why so scrawny, cat?
Starving for fat fish or mice . . .
Or backyard love?
BASHO

Dewdrop, let me cleanse
In your brief sweet waters . . .
These dark hands of life
BASHO

Lightning flash, crash . . .
Waiting in the bamboo grove
See three dew-drops fall
BUSON

Ashes my burnt hut . . .
But wonderful the cherry
Blooming on my hill
HOKUSHI

17

Life? butterfly
On a swaying grass that's all . . .
But exquisite!
SOIN

Glorious the moon . . .
Therefore our thanks dark clouds
Come to rest our necks
BASHO

What a peony . . .
Demanding to be measured
By my little fan!
ISSA

Under cherry-trees
Soup, the salad, fish and all . . .
Seasoned with petals
BASHO

Now from cherry-trees . . .
Millions of maidens flying
Fierce war-lord storm
SADAIYE

18

Moon so bright for love!
Come closer, quilt . . . enfold
My passionate cold!
SAMPU

Too curious flower
Watching us pass, met death . . .
Our hungry donkey
BASHO

Cloud of cherry-bloom . . .
Tolling twilight bell . . . Temple
Ueno? Asakura?
BASHO

Must springtime fade?
Then cry all birds . . . and fishes'
Cold pale eyes pour tears
BASHO

A nursemaid scarecrow . . .
Frightening the wind and sun
From playing baby
ISSA

ON HER DEAD SON

In what windy land
Wanders now my little dear
Dragonfly hunter?

CHIYO-NI

A saddening world:
Flowers whose sweet blooms must fall . . .
As we too, alas . . .

ISSA

Describe plum-blossoms?
Better than my verses . . . white
Wordless butterflies

REIKAN

Lend me water please?
Some fresh young morning-glory,
Careless . . . took my well

CHIYO-NI

A YOUNG SISTER

Pitiful . . . on my
Outstretched palm at dusk dies
The little firefly

KYORAI

You stupid scarecrow!
Under your very stick-feet
Birds are stealing beans!
YAYU

Afternoon shower . . .
Walking and talking in the street:
Umbrella and raincoat!
BUSON

In the farther field
A scarecrow kept me company . . .
Walking as I walked
SANIN

Pretty butterflies . . .
Be careful of pine-needle points
In this gusty wind!
SHUSEN

Ah, unrequited love!
Now elevate your chin and keen
Tom-cat, to the moon!
KYORAI

Hi! kids mimicking
Cormorants . . . you are more like
Real cormorants than they!
ISSA

Buzzing the bee trades
Peony for peony
With the butterfly
TAIGI

Such utter silence!
Even the crickets' singing . . .
Muffled by hot rocks
BASHO

Far across low mist
Intermittently the lake
Lifts a snow-white sail
GAKOKU

A white swan swimming . . .
Parting with her unmoved breast
Cherry-petaled pond
ROKA

22

For a cool evening
I hired the old temple porch . . .
Penny in the dish
SHIKI

Quite a hundred gourds
Sprouting from the fertile soul . . .
Of a single vine
CHIYO-NI

Swallow in the dusk . . .
Spare my little buzzing friends
Among the flowers
BASHO

Old dark sleepy pool . . .
Quick unexpected frog
Goes plop! Watersplash!
BASHO

My shadowy path
I've swept all day and now . . . oh no!
Camellia-shower!
YAHA

Hard the beggar's bed . . .
But sociable and busy
With insect-talking

CHIYO-NI

Come come! Come out!
From bogs old frogs command the dark
And look . . . the stars!

KIKAKU

Over the mountain
Bright the full white moon now smiles . . .
On the flower-thief

ISSA

Starting to call you:
Come watch these butterflies . . .
Oh! I'm all alone

TAIGI

Good friend grasshopper
Will you play the caretaker
For my little grave?

ISSA

24

A lost child crying
Stumbling over the dark fields . . .
Catching fireflies
RYUSUI

The snake departed
But the little eyes that glared . . .
Dew, shining in the grass
KYOSHI

Ah! Brave dragon-fly . . .
Taking for your perch this swatter
Consecrate to death
KOHYO

I raised my knife to it:
Then walked empty-handed on . . .
Proud rose of Sharon
SAMPU

Giddy grasshopper
Take care . . . do not leap and crush
These pearls of dewdrop
ISSA

25

Darting dragon-fly . . .
Pull off its shiny wings and look . . .
Bright red pepper-pod
KIKAKU

REPLY:
Bright red pepper-pod . . .
It needs but shiny winds and look . . .
Darting dragon-fly!
BASHO

Tiny sentences
Brushing soft on my shutters . . .
Bush-clover voices
SESSHI

Mirror-pond of stars . . .
Suddenly a summer shower
Dimples the water
SORA

Sadness at twilight . . .
Villain! I have let my hand
Cut that peony
BUSON

In dim dusk and scent
A witness now half hidden . . .
Evenfall orchid

BUSON

Now be a good boy
Take good care of our house . . .
Cricket my child

ISSA

Wake! The sky is light!
Let us to the road again . . .
Companion butterfly!

BASHO

Stillness . . . then the bat
Flying among the willows
Black against green sky

KIKAKU

Now my loneliness
Following the fireworks . . .
Look! A falling star!

SHIKI

Stupid hot melons . . .
Rolling like fat idiots
Out from leafy shade!
KYORA

For morning-glories
I can foresee grave danger . . .
Single-stick practice
CHORA

Can't it get away
From the sticky pine-branches . . .
Cicada singing?
GIJOENS

Silent the old town . . .
The scent of flowers floating . . .
And evening bell
BASHO

Vendor of bright fans
Carrying his pack of breeze . . .
Suffocating heat!
SHIKI

Voices of two bells
That speak from twilight temples . . .
Ah! cool dialogue
BUSON

Deep in dark forest
A woodcutter's dull axe talking . . .
And a woodcutter
BUSON

Camellia-petal
Fell in silent dawn . . . spilling
A water-jewel
BASHO

In the twilight rain
These brilliant-hued hibiscus . . .
A lovely sunset
BASHO

Friend, that open mouth
Reveals your whole interior . . .
Silly hollow frog!
ANON.

Butterfly asleep
Folded soft on temple bell . . .
Then bronze gong rang!
BUSON

Good evening breeze!
Crooked and meandering
Your homeward journey
ISSA

See the morning breeze
Ruffling his so silky hair . . .
Cool caterpillar
BUSON

Oh lucky beggar! . . .
Bright heaven and cool earth
Your summer outfit
KIKAKU

The turnip farmer rose
And with a fresh-pulled turnip . . .
Pointed to my road
ISSA

FLOWER IN THE STREAM
Thus too my lovely life
Must end, another flower . . .
To fall and float away
ONITSURA

I am going out . . .
Be good and play together
My cricket children
ISSA

Not a voice or stir . . .
Darkness lies on fields and streets
Sad: the moon has set
IMOZENI

Lady butterfly
Perfumes her wings by floating
Over the orchid
BASHO

If strangers threaten
Turn into fat green bullfrogs . . .
Pond-cooling melons
ISSA

Yellow evening sun . . .
Long shadow of the scarecrow
Reaches to the road
SHOHA

A camellia
Dropped down into still waters
Of a deep dark well
BUSON

For the emperor
Himself he will not lift his hat . . .
A stiff-backed scarecrow
DANSUI

In the holy dusk
Nightingales begin their psalm . . .
Good! the dinner-gong!
BUSON

Live in simple faith . . .
Just as this trusting cherry
Flowers, fades, and falls
ISSA

Night is bright with stars . . .
Silly woman, whimpering:
Shall I light the lamp?
ETSUJIN

Black desolate moor . . .
I bow before the Buddha
Lighted in thunder
KAKEI

Dirty bath-water
Where can I pour you? . . . insects
Singing in the grass
ONITSURA

Wee bitter cricket
Crying all this sunny day . . .
Or is he laughing?
OEMARU

A short summer night . . .
But in this solemn darkness
One peony bloomed
BUSON

33

Long the summer day . . .
Patterns on the ocean sand . . .
Our idle footprints
SHIKI

Angry I strode home . . .
But stooping in my garden
Calm old willow-tree
RYOTA

Oh do not swat them . . .
Unhappy flies forever
Wringing their thin hands
ISSA

See . . . the heavy leaf
On the silent windless day . . .
Falls of its own will
BONCHO

Rash tom-cat lover . . .
Careless even of that rice
Stuck in your whiskers
TAIGI

34

Moon so bright for love!
Oh, hear the farmer by that light . . .
Flailing his lovely rice!
ETSUJIN

Now the swinging bridge
Is quieted with creepers . . .
Like our tendrilled life
BASHO

Dancing in my silks
Money tossed itself away . . .
Pretty, this paper dress!
SONO-JO

The sea darkening . . .
Oh voices of the wild ducks
Crying, whirling, white
BASHO

White moth, flutter off:
Fly back into my breast now
Quickly, my own soul!
WAFU

35

Nine times arising
To see the moon . . . whose solemn pace
Marks only midnight yet
BASHO

Watching, I wonder
What poet could put down his quill . . .
A pluperfect moon!
ONITSURA

Do your worst, old frost
You can no longer wound me . . .
Last chrysanthemum!
OEMARU

Pebbles shining clear,
And clear six silent fishes . . .
Deep autumn water
BUSON

A bright autumn moon . . .
In the shadow of each grass
An insect chirping
BUSON

You turn and suddenly
There in purpling autumn sky . . .
White Fujiami!
ONITSURA

Here, where a thousand
Captains swore grand conquest . . . tall
Grass their monument
BASHO

Yellow autumn moon . . .
Unimpressed the scarecrow stands
Simply looking bored
ISSA

White chrysanthemum . . .
Before that perfect flower
Scissors hesitate
BUSON

Cruel autumn wind
Cutting to the very bones . . .
Of my poor scarecrow
ISSA

Now in late autumn
Look, on my old rubbish-heap . . .
Blue morning-glory
TAIGI

A single cricket
Chirps, chirps, chirps, and is still . . . my
Candle sinks and dies
ANON.

Firewords ended
And spectators gone away . . .
Ah, how vast and dark!
SHIKI

Two ancient pine-trees . . .
A pair of gnarled and sturdy hands
With ten green fingers
RYOTO

I must turn over . . .
Beware of local earthquakes
Bedfellow cricket!
ISSA

38

Oh! I ate them all
And oh! What a stomach-ache . . .
Green stolen apples
SHIKI

Now in sad autumn
As I take my darkening path . . .
A solitary bird
BASHO

At our last parting
Bending between boat and shore . . .
That weeping willow
SHIKI

At Furue in rain
Gray water and gray sand . . .
Picture without lines
BUSON

Oh sorry tom-cat
Bigger blacker knights of love
Have knocked you out!
SHIKO

The old fisherman
Unalterably intent . . .
Cold evening rain
BUSON

While I turned my head
That traveler I'd just passed . . .
Melted into mist
SHIKI

Visiting the graves . . .
Trotting on to show the way . . .
Old family dog
ISSA

Will we meet again
Here at your flowering grave . . .
Two white butterflies?
BASHO

So enviable . . .
Maple-leaves most glorious
Contemplating death
SHIKO

Shocking . . . the red of
Lacquered fingernails against
A white chrysanthemum
CHIYO-NI

Dry cheerful cricket
Chirping, keeps the autumn gay . . .
Contemptuous of frost
BASHO

Deepen, drop, and die
Many-hued chrysanthemums . . .
One black earth for all
RYUSUI

Before boiled chestnuts
Cross-legged lad is squatting . . .
Carved wooden Buddha
ISSA

Defeated in the fray
By bigger battlers for love . . .
Tom-cat seeks a mouse
SHIKO

Asking their road . . .
Seven yellow bamboo hats
All turned together
ANON.

Torches! Come and see
The burglar I have captured . . .
Oh! My eldest son!
SOKAN

Autumn mosquitoes
Buzz me, bite me . . . see, I am
Long prepared for death
SHIKI

Nice: wild persimmons . . .
And notice how the mother
Eats the bitter parts
ISSA

Gray marsh, black cloud . . .
Flapping away in autumn rain
Last old slow heron
ANON.

42

First white snow of fall
Just enough to bend the leaves
Of faded daffodils
BASHO

What a gorgeous one
That fat sleek huge old chestnut
I could not get at . . .
ISSA

None broke the silence . . .
Nor visitor nor host . . . nor
White chrysanthemum
RYOTA

If you were silent
Flight of herons on dark sky . . .
Oh! Autumn snowflakes!
SOKAN

Chilling autumn rain . . .
The moon, too bright for showers,
Slips from their fingers
TOKUKU

Rainy-month, dripping
On and on as I lie abed . . .
Ah, old man's memories!
BUSON

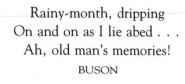

November sunrise . . .
Uncertain, the cold storks stand . . .
Bare sticks in water
KAKEI

From dark windy hills
Voices driving weary horses . . .
Shouting of the storm
KYOKUSUI

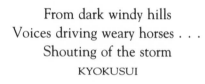

Slanting lines of rain . . .
On the dusty samisen
A mouse is trotting
BUSON

Oh former renter
I know it all, all . . . down to
The very cold you felt
ISSA

Gray moor, unmarred
By any path . . . a single branch . . .
A bird . . . November
ANON.

Lonely umbrella
Passing the house at twilight . . .
First snow falling soft
YAHA

Carven gods long gone . . .
Dead leaves alone foregather
On the temple porch
BASHO

Five or six of us
Remain, huddled together . . .
Bent old willow-trees
KYORAI

Plume of pampas grass
Trembling in every wind . . .
Hush, my lonely heart
ISSA

Tea-water, tired
Waiting while we watched the snow . . .
Froze itself a hat
SOKAN

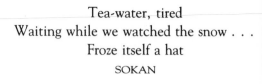

Cold first winter rain . . .
Poor monkey, you too could use
A little woven cape
BASHO

Winter rain deepens
Lichened letters on the grave . . .
And my old sadness
ROKA

Cold winter shower . . .
See all the people running
Across seta bridge!
JOSO

Old weary willows . . .
I thought how long the road would be
When you went away
BUSON

46

No oil to read by . . .
I am off to bed but ah! . . .
My moonlit pillow
BASHO

Descending seaward
Far-off mountain waterfall . . .
Winter nights are still
KYOKUSUI

All heaven and earth
Flowered white obliterate . . .
Snow . . . unceasing snow
HASHIN

Considerate dogs . . .
Stepping off into the snow
As I walk the path
ISSA

But when I halted
On the windy street at twilight . . .
Snow struck against me
KITO

47

Call him back! Ah no,
He's blown from sight already . . .
Fish-peddler in the snow
ANON.

Crossing it alone
In cold moonlight . . . the brittle bridge
Echoes my footsteps
TAIGI

Such a little child
To send to be a priestling
Icy poverty
SHIKI

Windy winter rain . . .
My silly big umbrella
Tries walking backward
SHISEI-JO

Buddha on the hill . . .
From your holy nose indeed
Hangs an icicle
ISSA

This snowy morning
That black crow I hate so much . . .
But he's beautiful!
BASHO

Look at the candle!
What a hungry wind it is . . .
Hunting in the snow!
SEIRA

If there were fragrance
These heavy snow-flakes settling . . .
Lilies on the rocks
BASHO

Ah! I intended
Never never to grow old . . .
Listen: New Year's bell!
JOKUN

Snow-swallowed valley:
Only the winding river . . .
Black fluent brush-stroke
BONCHO

Roaring winter storm
Rushing to its utter end . . .
Ever-sounding sea
GONSUI

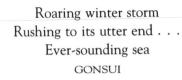

Eleven brave knights
Canter through the whirling snow . . .
Not one bends his neck
SHIKI

Going snow-viewing
One by one the walkers vanish . . .
Whitely falling veils
KATSURI

"Yes, come in!" I cried . . .
But at the windy snow-hung gate
Knocking still went on
KYORAI

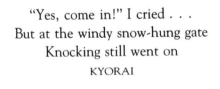

See: surviving suns
Visit the ancestral grave . . .
Bearded, with bent canes
BASHO

THE ORPHAN SPEAKS:
The year-end party . . .
I am even envious
Of scolded children
ISSA

I gave the greetings
Of the bright New Year . . . as though
I held a plum-branch
SHIKI

On jolly New Year's Day
My last year's bills drop in
To pay their compliments
ANON.

DEATH-SONG:
Leaf alone, fluttering
Alas, leaf alone, fluttering . . .
Floating down the wind
ANON.

DEATH-SONG:
I have known lovers . . .
Cherry-bloom . . . the nightingale . . .
I will sleep content
ANON.

51

DEATH-SONG:
Fever-felled half-way,
My dreams arose to march again . . .
Into a hollow land
BASHO

DEATH-SONG:
Three loveliest things:
Moonlight . . . cherry-bloom . . . now I go
Seeking silent snow
RIPPO

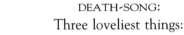

Such a fine first dream . . .
But they laughed at me . . . they said
I had made it up
TAKUCHI

Even my plain wife . . .
Exquisite as visitors
On New Year's morning
ISO

New year gift-giving . . .
Ah, baby at her bare breast
Reaching tiny hands
ISSA

52

First wind of the year . . .
The oil-lamp in the washroom
Shudders and is still
OEMARU

Felicitations!
Still . . . I guess this year too
Will prove only so-so
ISSA

First dream of the year . . .
I kept it a dark secret . . .
Smiling to myself
SHO-U

Sun-melted snow . . .
With my stick I guide this great
Dangerous river
ISSA

From my tiny roof
Smooth . . . soft . . . still-white snow
Melts in melody
ISSA

Icicles and water
Old differences dissolved . . .
Drip down together
TEISHITSU

Old snow is melting . . .
Now the huts unfreezing too
Free all the children
ISSA

A childless housewife . . .
How tenderly she touches
Little dolls for sale
RANSETSU

Now wild geese return . . .
What draws them crying crying
All the long dark night?
ROKA

Pouring floods of rain . . .
Won't Mount Fuji wash away
To a muddy lake?
BUSON

54

Clear-colored stones
Are vibrating in the brook-bed . . .
Or the water is
SOSEKI

In my new clothing
I feel so different I must
Look like someone else
BASHO

Oh you bawdy breeze . . .
Thatcher bending on the roof
I see the bottom!
ISSA

Immobile Fuji . . .
Alone unblanketed by
Millions of new leaves
BUSON

Spring morning marvel . . .
Lovely namesless little hill
On a sea of mist
BASHO

Passing the doll shop
I picked up the littlest one . . .
Suddenly I smiled

BAISHITSU

There in the water
Color of the water moves . . .
Translucent fishes

RAIZAN

Hazy ponded moon
And pale night sky are broken . . .
Bungling black frog

BUSON

Silver-soft riverside . . .
Dim splash of far-thrown net . . .
Fishing for the moon?

TAIGI

Paper-weights protect
Gay picture-books in the shop . . .
Inquisitive breeze

KITO

Ah-ah-ah-choo! That
Spring catarrh! . . . now I've lost sight
Of my first skylark
YAYU

An April shower . . .
See that thirsty mouse lapping
River Sumida
ISSA

Rainfall in April . . .
Tears from out weeping willow . . .
Petals from our plum
SHOHA

Ah little warbler . . .
Thanks-droppings on my porch
Because I love you?
BASHO

Under my tree-roof
Slanting lines of April rain
Separate to drops
BASHO

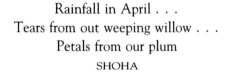

Farmer, raise your head . . .
Direct this stranger who will smile
And disappear
BUSON

Good morning, sparrow . . .
Writing on my clean veranda
With your dewy feet
SHIKI

Beach fishermen go
Bobbing out . . . Beach poppies stay
Bending with sea-breeze
KYORAI

Even the ocean
Rising and falling all day . . .
Sighing green like trees
BUSON

I could not see him
That fluttering fly-off bird . . .
But the plum-petals . . .
SHIKI

Gliding river boat . . .
Rising skylarks . . . rippling sounds
To our right and left
RANKO

Bird-droppings pattern
The purples and the yellows of
My iris petals

Shining on the sea . . .
Dazzling sunlight shaking over
Hills of cherry-bloom
BUSON

Over the low hedge
Honest plum distributes petals
Half inside . . . half out
CHORA

Riverbank plum-tree . . .
Do your reflected blossoms
Really flow away?
BUSON

Blue evening sea . . .
From spring islands near and far
New lights are shining
SHIKI

The old messenger
Proffering his plum-branch first . . .
Only then the letter
KIKAKU

Midnight full of stars . . .
Dim cherry-petals floating on
Rice-paddy waters
BUSON

Over my shoulder . . .
My friends who followed me were lost
In clouds of blossom
CHORA

The seashore temple . . .
Incoming rollers flow in time
To the holy flute
BUSON

Low-tide morning . . .
The willow's skirts are trailed
In stinking mud
BASHO

Here comes Mr. Horse . . .
Quick, quick, out of the roadway
Happy Sparrowlet
ISSA

Moonlight stillness
Lights the petals falling . . . falling . . .
On the silenced lute
SHIKI

Green . . . green . . . green . . .
Willow-leaf threads are sliding
River-running-water
ONITSURA

Cherry-petal days . . .
Birds with two legs glitter now
Horses gleam with four
ONITSURA

Heat-wavelets rising . . .
Plum-petals drifting wavering
Down on burning rocks
SHIKI

Come now, play with me . . .
Fatherless motherless dear
Little sparrow-child
ISSA

No bold rain-cloud for
A hundred miles around . . . dares
Brave the peonies
BUSON

In the clear fording
Pale feet of the silent girl . . .
Clouding May waters
BUSON

Opening thin arms . . .
A pink peony big as this!
Said my bitty girl
ISSA

62

Ultra-pink peony . . .
Silver siamese soft-cat . . .
Gold-dust butterfly . . .
BUSON

Energetic ant . . .
Silhouetted on the still
Snowflake-peony
BUSON

In the yard plum-trees
Blossom . . . in the brothel
Girls are buying obis
BUSON

That white peony . . .
Lover of the moon trembling
Now at twilight
GYODAI

Facing the candle
The peony also burning . . .
Motionless as death
KYOROKU

The first firefly . . .
But he got away and I . . .
Air in my fingers
ISSA

Listen, all you fleas . . .
You can come on pilgrimage, o k . . .
But then, off you git!
ISSA

But if I held it . . .
Could I touch the lightness of this
Flutter-butterfly?
BUSON

Hanging sadly down
Amid the merry-makers . . .
Green weeping willow
ROKA SHONIN

Out of my way please
And let me plant my bamboos . . .
Old brother toad
CHORA

64

For that brief moment
When the firefly went out . . . O
The lonely darkness
HOKUSHI

Now this old poet
Emerges from the purple depths
Of the convolvulus
CHORA

Pinions pulsating . . .
Your mind traveling afar
Butterfly dreamer?
CHIYO-NI

Moon-in-the-water . . .
Broken-again . . . broken-again . . .
Still a solid seal
CHOSU

Now having taken
Warmed water . . . the vase welcomes
My Camellia
ONITSURA

Fallen now to earth
After dancing journeyings . . .
Kite that lost its soul
KUBONTA

Keeping company
With us, pigeons and sparrows . . .
Low-tide-lookers all
ISSA

What, traveling
In the rain? . . . but where can he
Be wending snailward?
ISSA

With my new clothing
Alas . . . spring has been buried
In that wooden chest
SAIKAKU

Hands upon the ground
Old aristocratic frog
Recites his poem
SOKAN

66

As I picked it up
To cage it . . . the firefly
Lit my finger-tips
TAIGI

Fleeing the hunter
The firefly took cover . . .
The evening moon
RYOTA

Softly folded fawn
Shivers, shaking off the butterfly . . .
And sleeps again
ISSA

The heavy wagon
Shook all the roadside . . . waking
A single butterfly
SHOHA

In the golden room
Frightened quick calligraphy . . .
Escaping swallow
BUSON

He wades the river
Carrying the girl and see . . .
Carrying the moon
SHIKI

For deliciousness
Try fording this rivulet . . .
Sandals in one hand
BUSON

Elegant singer
Would you further favor us
With a dance . . . . o frog?
ISSA

Before the sacred
Mountain shrine of Kamiji . . .
My head bent itself
ISSA

Rainy afternoon . . .
Little daughter you will never
Teach that cat to dance
ISSA

On the low-tide beach
Everything we stoop to pick . . .
Moves in our fingers
CHIYO-NI

Flower-petal fell . . .
Then the rooster crowed, and see . . .
Another petal
BAISHITSU

Dark the well at dawn . . .
Rising with the first bucket . . .
Camellia-blossom
KAKEI

Now take this flea:
He simply cannot jump . . . and
I love him for it
ISSA

The floating heron
Pecks at it till it shatters . . .
Full-moon-on-water
ZUIRYU

For a companion
On my walking trip . . . perhaps
A little butterfly
SHIKI

Ah good Buddhist frog . . .
Rising to a clearer light
By non-attachment
JOSO

Bats come out at dusk . . .
Woman over the way . . . why
Do you stare at me?
BUSON

Overhanging pine . . .
Adding its mite of needles
To the waterfall
BASHO

Squads of frogs jumped in
When they heard the plunk-plash
Of a single frog
WAKYU

Little silver fish
Pointing upstream moving downstream
In clear quick water
SOSEKI

Look . . . the palace . . .
You can glimpse it through that hole
In the mosquito-fog
ISSA

Congratulations
Issa! . . . you have survived to feed
This year's mosquitoes
ISSA

In your summer-room . . .
Garden and mountain going too
As we slowly walk
BASHO

Just beyond the smoke
Of our smudge this evening . . .
Mosquito-music
SHIRAO

Do I hear voices
From far lands above the clouds?
O . . . silly skylarks

KYOROKU

Shortest summer night . . .
In early morning lamps still
Burning on the bay

SHIKI

Moon-in-the-water
Turned a white somersault . . . yes
And went floating off

RYOTA

Even fly-swatting
By these border guards . . . O how
Vicious and correct

TAIGI

Quick-pattering rain . . .
Chance and vanity dictate
Gay impromptu hats

OTSUYU

You hear that fat frog
In the seat of honor, singing
Bass? . . . that's the boss
ISSA

Windy-web spider
What is your silent speaking . . .
Your unsung song?
BASHO

And each morning
Right above this little roof . . .
My private skylark
JOSO

Don't waste precious time
Now, tagging along with me . . .
Brother butterfly
ISSA

Experimenting . . .
I hung the moon on various
Branches of the pine
HOKUSHI

Swat softly softly
At the sick-room flies . . . because
I seek for sleep
SHIKI

The devoted clerk . . .
Not to waste a jot of breeze
Naps on a ledger pillow
ISSA

On his garden path
This sparrow scatters pebbles . . .
Man forgotten
SHOHA

River Mogami
Winding from northern mountains
Washes warm summer
SHIKI

Summer-night insects
Falling burnt and dead . . . upon
My poem's paper
SHIKI

74

You are just too late
To help me with the lamp . . . my moth
Light-extinguisher
ISSA

Again coolness comes . . .
Silver undersides of leaves
Evening-breeze blown
SHIKI

After that illness
My long gazing at roses
Wearied the eyelids
SHIKI

The night was hot . . .
Stripped to the waist the snail
Enjoyed the moonlight
ISSA

My summer illness . . .
But at last my life was spared
At the very bones
SHIKI

75

Careful, champion flea
And look before you leap . . .
Here's River Sumida
ISSA

Coming from the bath . . .
Cool on her breasts the warm breeze
Of the veranda
SHIKI

Fui! A sour plum . . .
Thin eyebrows pinched together
On the lovely face
BUSON

Holy noon duet:
Basso-snoring priest . . . devout
Contralto-cuckoo
SHIKI

Farther in the grove
The lantern walks . . . nearer nearer
Sings the nightingale
SHIKI

With the new clothes
Remember . . . the crow stays black
And the heron white
CHORA

I scooped up the moon
In my water bucket . . . and
Spilled it on the grass
RYUHO

Must you come to vex
My sick eyes that still can move . . .
Bed-criss-crossing fly?
SHIKI

Coolness on the bridge . . .
Moon, you and I alone
Unresigned to sleep
KIKUSHA-NI

In the endless rain
Is it turning sunward still . . .
Trusting hollyhock?
HASHO

77

Hot slow afternoon . . .
Suddenly the hand has stopped . . .
Slow-falling fan
TAIGI

In summer moonlight
They go visiting the graves . . .
Savoring the cool
ISSA

In the morning breezes,
Climbing in a single line
Go singing skylarks
RYOTA

A near nightingale . . .
But my head just couldn't fit
Through the lattices
YAHA

A summer shower . . .
Along all the street, servants
Slapping shut shutters
SHIKI

78

Rainfall and thunder
Beating on boards and blossoms . . .
Indiscriminate
SAMPO

Rain-obliterated . . .
The river, some roofs,
A bridge without a shore
BASHO

In lantern-light
My yellow chrysanthemums
Lost all their color
BUSON

Morning-misted street . . .
With white ink an artist brushes
A dream of people
BUSON

At Nara Temple . . .
Fresh-scented chrysanthemums
And ancient images
BASHO

An old tree was felled . . .
Echoing, dark echoing
Thunder in the Hills
MEISETSU

THE GREAT FIRE OF KANDA
Heat-waves to heaven . . .
Rising from the ruined hearts of
Three thousand homes
SHIKI

Chanting at the altar
Of the inner sanctuary . . .
A cricket priest
ISSA

Sad twilight cricket . . .
Yes, I have wasted once again
Those daylight hours
RIKEI

A sudden shower . . .
Terrified, loud idiot ducks
High-tailing home
KIKAKU

80

My melons that you
Stole last year . . . this year I place
Upon your grave, my son
OEMARU

On these rainy days
That old poet Ryokan
Wallows in self-pity
RYOKAN

Pitiful . . . fearful . . .
These poor scarecrows look like men
In autumn moonlight
SHIKI

We stand still to hear
Tinkle of far temple bell . . .
Willow-leaves falling
BASHO

The evening breezes . . .
Water lapping lightly on
The heron's leg-sticks
BUSON

The wet kingfisher
Shakes his feathers in the late
Reflected sunlight
TORI

In unending rain
The house-pent boy is fretting
With his brand-new kite
SHOHA

The calling bell
Travels the curling mist-ways . . .
Autumn morning
BASHO

Nightlong in the cold
That monkey sits conjecturing
How to catch the moon
SHIKI

Dark unending night . . .
Once, outside the paper screen,
A lantern passing
SHIKI

They have gone . . . but
They lit the garden lantern
Of their little house
SHIKI

On one riverbank
Sunbeams slanting down . . . but on
The other . . . raindrops
BUSON

Supper in autumn . . .
Flat light through an open door
From a setting sun
CHORA

September sunshine . . .
The hovering dragonfly's
Shimmering shadow
KARO

Do I dare depend
Upon you for firm friendship
Dear morning-glory?
BASHO

A windblown grass . . .
Hovering mid-air in vain
An autumn dragonfly
BASHO

Now the old scarecrow
Looks just like other people . . .
Drenching autumn rain
SEIBI

Here is the dark tree
Denuded now of leafage . . .
But a million stars
SHIKI

Up from my illness
I went to the chrysanthemums . . .
How cold they smelled!
OTSUJI

Waking in the night
Ladded my autumn coughing
To insect voices
JOSO

84

Jagged candle-flame . . .
The very shape of autumn sifts
Through the shutters
RAIZAN

Urging on my horse
Into mist-blanketed water . . .
River-gurgle sounds
TAIGI

White chrysanthemums
Making all else about them
Reflected riches
CHORA

Peacefulness . . . today
Fujiama stands above us
Mist-invisible
BASHO

Smack-ack . . . smack-ack . . .
Men driving fish-net stakes
In white-fog morning
BUSON

White autumn moon . . .
Black-branch shadow-patterns
Printed on the mats
KIKAKU

Exquisite the dewy
Bramble . . . to every thorn
A single droplet
BUSON

From the temple steps
I lift to the autumn moon
My veritable face
BASHO

In this solid mist
What are those people shouting
Between boat and hill?
KITO

Nights are getting cold . . .
Not a single insect now
Attacks the candle
SHIKI

His hat blown off . . .
How pitiless the pelting
Storm on the scarecrow

HAGI-JO

In my own village
I think there are more scarecrows left
Than other people

CHASEI

Swallows flying south . . .
My house too of sticks and paper
Only a stopping-place

KYORAI

After moon-viewing
My companionable shadow
Walked along with me

SODO

After the windstorm
Foraging for firewood . . .
Three fierce old women

BUSON

Roadside barley-stalks
Torn by our clutching fingers . . .
As we smiled farewell
BASHO

Suddenly chill fall . . .
Why should that ragged fortune-teller
Look so surprised?
BUSON

All the world is cold . . .
My fishing-line is trembling
In the autumn wind
BUSON

Autumn breezes shake
The scarlet flowers my poor child
Could not wait to pick
ISSA

Seeking in my hut
For unlocked midnight treasures . . .
A cricket burglar
ISSA

Little orphan girl . . .
Eating a lonely dinner
In winter twilight
SHOHAKU

In the wintry moon
Gales raging down the river
Hone the rock-edges
CHORA

The new-laid garden . . .
Rocks settling in harmony
In soft winter rain
SHADO

When I raised my head . . .
There was my rigid body
Lying bitter cold
SEIBI

Over wintry fields
Bold sparrow companies fly
Scarecrow to scarecrow
SAZANAMI

Bath-tub firewood . . .
Thanks for this final service
Faithful old scarecrow
JOSO

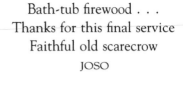

My very bone-ends
Made contact with the icy quilts
Of deep December
BUSON

Poor thin crescent
Shivering and twisted high . . .
In the bitter dark
ISSA

So lonely . . . lovely . . .
The exquisite pure-white fan
Of the girl I lost
BUSON

In winter moonlight
A clear look at my old hut . . .
Dilapidated
ISSA

Black calligraphy
Of geese . . . pale printed foothills . . .
For a seal, full moon
BUSON

In my dark winter
Lying ill . . . at last I ask
How fares my neighbor?
BASHO

The old dog lies intent
Listening . . . does he overhear
The burrowing moles?
ISSA

A thousand roof-tops
A thousand market-voices . . .
Winter-morning mist
BUSON

First snow last night . . .
There across the morning bay
Sudden mountain-white
SHIKI

When the waterpot
Burst that silent night with cold . . .
My eyes split open
BASHO

Winter having touched
These fields . . . the very tomtits
Perch on the scarecrow
KIKAKU

Cold winter rainfall . . .
Mingling all their gleaming horns
Oxen at the fence
RANKO

See the red berries . . .
Fallen like little footprints
On the garden snow
SHIKI

Winter-evening snow . . .
The uncompleted bridge is all
An arch of whiteness
BASHO

Moonlit snowfields . . .
Here the bloodied samurai
Cast their noble lives
KIKAKU

Midnight wanderer
Walking through the snowy street . . .
Echoing dog-bark
SHIKI

As to icicles
I often wonder why they grow
Some long . . . some short
ONITSURA

In winter moonlight
Fish-net stakes cast their shifting
Uneven shadows
SHIRAO

Colder far than snow . . .
Winter moonlight echoing on
My whitened hair
JOSO

So close . . . so vast . . .
Rattling winter hailstones on
My umbrella-hat
BASHO

Long-walking lantern
Disappeared into some house . . .
Desolate white hills
SHIKI

Solitary crow . . .
Companioning my progress
Over snowy fields
SENNA

Staring delighted
Even at walking horses
In new morning snow
BASHO

Blinding wild snow
Blows, whirls and drifts about me . . .
In this world alone
CHORA

94

Winter moonlight casts
Cold tree-shadows long and still . . .
My warm one moving
SHIKI

In that cold darkness
My horse stumbled suddenly
Just outside the house
BUSON

Look at that stray cat
Sleeping . . . snug under the eaves
In the whistling snow
TAIGI

In my new-year heart
I feel no fury . . . even at
These tramplers of snow
YAYU

Coffin and mourners
Passed me walking down the street . . .
Midnight at New Year's
SHIKI

To celebrate New Year's
We feast newly-opened eyes on
Snowy Fujiama
SOKAN

Poet nightingale . . .
Will I hear your later verses
In the vale of death?
ANON.

DEATH-SONG:

Suddenly you light
And as suddenly go dark . . .
Fellow-firefly
CHINE-JO

DEATH-SONG:

Full-moon and flowers
Solacing my forty-nine
Foolish years of song
ISSA

DEATH-SONG:

If they ask for me
Say: he had some business
In another world
SOKAN